Count Your Way through Canada

by Jim Haskins

illustrations by Steve Michaels

Carolrhoda Books, Inc./Minneapolis

To Michael and Marcus

Text copyright © 1989 by Jim Haskins
Illustrations copyright © 1989 by Carolrhoda Books, Inc.

This book is available in two editions:
Library binding by Carolrhoda Books, Inc.
Soft cover by First Avenue Editions
241 First Avenue North
Minneapolis, Minnesota 55401

LIBRARY OF CONGRESS CATALOGING-IN-PUBLICATION DATA

Haskins, James, 1941-
    Count your way through Canada / by Jim Haskins ; illustrations by
Steve Michaels.
        p.   cm.
    Summary: Presents the numbers one to ten in French, using each
number to introduce concepts about Canada and its culture.
    ISBN 0-87614-350-8 (lib. bdg.)
    ISBN 0-87614-515-2 (pbk.)
    1. Canada—Civilization—Juvenile literature. 2. Counting—
Juvenile literature. [1. Canada. 2. Counting.] I. Michaels,
Steve, ill. II. Title.
F1021.H37   1989
971—dc19   88-25898
                                                               CIP
                                                                AC

Manufactured in the United States of America

  2   3   4   5   6   7   8   9   10   99   98   97   96   95   94   93   92   91   90

Introductory Note

The major language of Canada is English, but several other languages are spoken there as well. In the northern regions, one can hear the languages of the Inuit (Eskimos) and of the various Indian tribes whose people were the first to live in the area now called Canada.

French is the native language of nearly one-third of all Canadians. It is the official language of the Canadian province of Quebec.

The French language uses the same alphabet as English. It also has the same basic sentence structure, the same placement of nouns and verbs. Pronunciation is very different, though. Written French uses accents, or marks, above some letters to show how they should be pronounced. But there are no accents in the written numbers one through ten in French.

1 un (uh)

One animal, the beaver, is most responsible for the European settlement of Canada. Around the middle of the 16th century, European hatmakers discovered that beaver fur made fine hats. The inner fur of the beaver has a very silky, shiny finish. Tall, floppy-brimmed hats made from beaver skins became very popular in Europe. French fur traders came to Canada and set up trading posts. They bought beaver furs from the Indians. By the 1630s, the colony of New France had been established along the St. Lawrence River. The colony's main town was named Quebec. The name comes from the Algonquian Indian word *kebec*, which means "place where the river narrows."

Today, the beaver appears on Canada's five-cent piece.

2 deux (duh)

Canada has **two** official languages, English and French. In the province of Quebec, street signs are printed in both languages. National government leaders are almost always bilingual, or able to speak two languages.

After many years of fighting, France surrendered its Canadian colony to England in 1763. But with the Quebec Act of 1774, England gave the French people of Quebec the right to keep their traditions, customs, and language, and to practice the Catholic religion, which at the time was banned in England.

3 trois (trwa)

There are oceans on **three** sides of Canada: the Atlantic Ocean to the east, the Pacific Ocean to the west, and the Arctic Ocean to the north. Canada is huge. It is the second largest country in the world. To go all the way across Canada, you have to pass through six different time zones.

Much of Canada is wilderness. The northern areas are so cold most of the year that only a small number of people live in them. Most Canadians live in less than two percent of Canada's territory.

Pacific Ocean

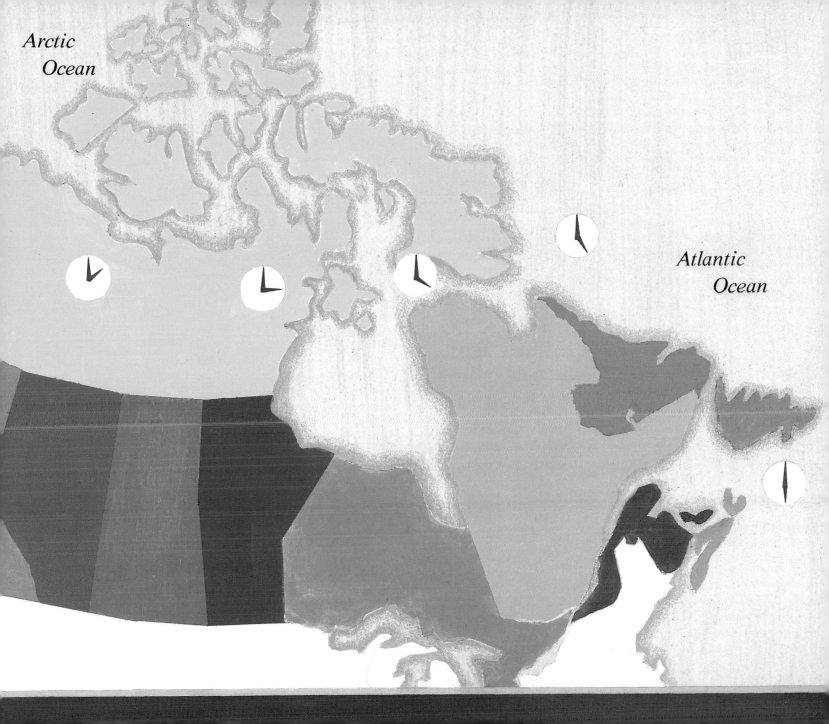

4 quatre (KAT're)

The flag of the province of Quebec has **four** *fleurs-de-lis* (flur-de-LEE), or lily flowers. The fleur-de-lis is a symbol of France because it was a design used by French kings. On the flag of Quebec the flowers surround a white cross, which is a symbol of the Christian faith. Many French Canadians are strong Catholics.

The flag is very much like the one that the French navigator Jacques Cartier brought to the colony of New France and that fur-trading ships flew as they crossed the Atlantic Ocean.

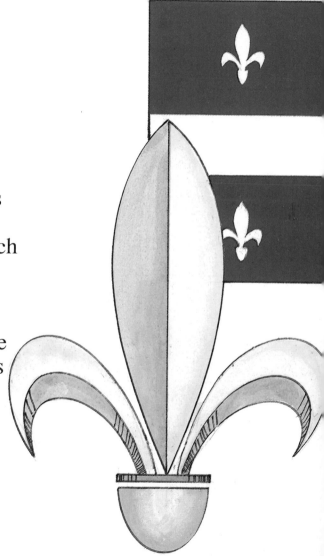

5

cinq
(sank)

There are **five** points, or main sections, to the maple leaf, which is the national symbol of Canada. There are huge maple tree forests in the southern part of the country, and maple-sugar candies in the shape of maple leaves are a Canadian product familiar to many Americans. In 1965, Canada adopted a national flag containing a red maple leaf on a white background, bordered by two red panels.

The maple leaf is on Canadian coins. It is the symbol of Air Canada, the national airline. One of Canada's major-league hockey teams is called the Toronto Maple Leafs.

6 six (seece)

There are **six** players on an ice hockey team. This sport started in Canada during the 19th century. It is a national winter pastime in Canada. There are many ice rinks available for practice. Although the sport became popular in the United States early in this century and there are a number of professional hockey teams in major U.S. cities, most players on U.S. hockey teams are Canadians.

7 sept (set)

Seven Canadian artists started the first art movement, or special way of painting, in Canada. They called themselves the Group of Seven. Every autumn, they set out together in a railway boxcar and traveled through the Canadian wilderness painting landscapes in bold, bright colors. Many of their works are on display in the new National Gallery of Canada in Ottawa.

8 huit (weet)

A traditional Inuit (IN-oo-it) costume for winter includes **eight** pieces of clothing: a shirt, a pair of leggings, two moccasin boots, two mittens, a hat, and a hooded robe. Such an outfit is made from eight to ten deer skins.

The people commonly called Eskimos call themselves the Inuit, which means simply "the people." Many of them live in the northernmost regions of Canada, on the barren, ice-covered land of the Arctic.

9 neuf (nuhf)

Nine activities at the annual Quebec Winter Carnival—the world's biggest winter celebration—are sliding, skiing, skating, snowshoeing, horse racing on ice, sleigh riding, tobogganing, parading, and snow sculpting.

The large and elaborate snow sculptures help to make this carnival special. Teams of snow sculptors come from all over the world to compete in the International Snow Sculpture Competition.

10 dix (deece)

Ten cannons point outward from the Royal Battery, which defended the old city of Quebec against the British in 1759. In later years, these fortifications were lost under docks and warehouses that were built along the St. Lawrence River. But the Battery was completely rebuilt in 1977 and now looks much as it did more than 200 years ago.

The old part of Quebec is like a museum. Walking through it is like walking through an old city in Europe long ago.

Pronunciation Guide

1 / **un** / uh

2 / **deux** / duh

3 / **trois** / trwa

4 / **quatre** / KAT're

5 / **cinq** / sank

6 / **six** / seece

7 / **sept** / set

8 / **huit** / weet

9 / **neuf** / nuhf

10 / **dix** / deece